TITLE I

PATH OF

HUNTERS

PATH OF HUNTERS

Animal Struggle in a Meadow

by

Robert Newton Peck

illustrations by Betty Fraser

Alfred A. Knopf   New York

THIS IS A BORZOI BOOK PUBLISHED BY ALFRED A. KNOPF, INC.

Library of Congress Cataloging in Publication Data
Peck, Robert. Path of hunters SUMMARY: Describes the behavior of a variety of common field, wood, and water animals emphasizing their interdependency for survival. 1. Animals, Habits and behavior of—Juvenile literature. [1. Animals—Habits and behavior] I. Fraser, Betty, illus. II. Title. PZ10.P415Pat 591.5 70-39596
ISBN 0-394-82424-5 ISBN 0-394-92424-X (Lib. Ed.)

Book design by Elliot Epstein
Manufactured in the United States of America
First Edition

To every child who has never seen the wintering of a stoat into an ermine.

To every boy who has yet to follow the webbed track of a snowshoe hare in fresh snow.

To every little girl who would love to stampede a herd of aphids in white birch or hear the merry whistle of a marmot to his mate. Or see a litter of newborn shrew, or taste the bittersweet honey from the combs of yellow jackets. Or watch a bracken unfurl, or sow a seed.

To the many creatures who gratefully enjoy the rightness of this brutal and beautiful order of things that was Created to work so well.

And to my Mother, who had squirrels in the kitchen.

Preface

Quick!

Run to the kitchen, look out the window, and then come back. The book can wait.

Well, what did you see? Nothing. At least you didn't see any animals except maybe a dog or a cat.

But there are lots of animals outdoors—so many birds and bugs and beasts that you actually have your own zoo. And that's what this story is about . . . all the animals that you hardly ever see who live near you.

This book is full of fighting. Because to live is to be hungry, and a hungry animal must hunt and kill, so many a smaller creature has to fight or run to stay alive.

You must kill, too. Before you eat a hotdog, you must kill a pig. But even if you yourself do not kill the pig, you are a meat-eater. You are a killer, just like the animals who each night prowl the jungle of your backyard.

But as you discover these creatures, you'll see that they are all more than killers. They love their mates and love their young. But most of all, they love just being alive . . . to play tag, juggle an acorn, or slide down a snowbank.

As you meet them in person, one by one in your backyard, you will know more than you ever knew before about your own life.

PATH OF
HUNTERS

One

It was not quite morning.

But the fat brown beetle roused himself, crawling from his bed which was an earth hole beneath a leaf. Hunching his tiny back, he performed an act very close to being a stretch. His day had begun because the hunger in his belly was too sharp to permit sleep, too painful to allow him to want anything but food. As he loosened up for a day of hunting, the hard shell wing covers of his back divided, so he could fan his soft, transparent flight wings and make them purr.

He did not fly. Instead he took a few casual steps from his bed. But then he stopped, his entire body rigid in concentration and all six of his feet braced for action. Nearby he had detected a faint scratching. Pausing only a second, he quickly ran to a willow root that had arched to the ground surface. Pawing the dirt furiously, the beetle uncovered a small white grub wriggling against the root, and captured it in his jaws. The grub fought to escape, but to no avail. He was immediately killed and rapturously eaten by the brown beetle.

In less than ten minutes the beetle had completely devoured the white grub, and now his only thought was to find another. One single grub is hardly a hearty meal for a beetle whose appetite demands several. His hunger stimulated by the grub's savory flavor, he waddled off through the grass in search of more food, wetting the shell of his back with shiny morning dew. He so blended with the glisten of grass and the dark April earth that an early-rising flicker, pecking in the willow tree above, overlooked the beetle's presence.

With a graceful dive, the flicker launched himself aloft to seek his breakfast. He banked sharply in flight, and his taillight of feathers flashed a brilliant white as he left his willow tree behind, heading toward the small freshwater pond beyond the meadow.

The black bat was at the pond, too. And though the sun was now almost fully up, she was still hungry. Her predawn hunting flight had not gone well for her, and there was good reason. Clinging to her as she flew was her one male offspring. He was just three days old, and since his birth he had attached himself firmly to his dam by sinking his sharp milkteeth deep into the false nipples near her groin.

The added weight of her son made the black bat slower; her flying was not its usual ballet of perfection. Already she was tired, but she did not want to return to her roost with an empty gullet to nag at her all day. So she frantically sought the bugs at the pond, flying along the surface of the water.

Perhaps it was caused by her fatigue, or the weight of her offspring, or the desperate ache of her hunger . . . but the bat misjudged her distance from the pond's surface. It was a stupid error. Mother and son plunged into the cold, dark water with a stinging *slap!*

Lying in the mud at the bottom of the pond, the giant snapping turtle had been sleeping. Though he was a groggy, slow-moving brute, he was instantly aware of the impact. His interest was sharpened by the soft, helpless splashing that followed.

Rousing himself from the mud and decaying leaves, the snapping turtle moved slowly through the black water toward the place where the bats had splashed down. He too was hungry. The big bullfrog he had caught two days ago was the last thing he had eaten. He could taste the reacting juices in his empty belly, juices that could reduce a pair of bats to pulp in a matter of minutes. So on he swam through the darkness, encouraged by the desperate sound of fluttery splashing that grew louder as he drew closer.

With an awkward flapping stroke, the mother bat bore her son along the surface of the pond, fighting her way through the cold water. She was a poor swimmer, and she was unaware of the giant snapping turtle approaching from beneath. She had become careless for an instant and had flown into what she could not now fly from. Her element was a dark sky, and not dark water.

Closer and closer to shore the mother bat paddled, struggling to keep her son's head as well as her own above the surface. Several times her delicate, sensitive nose filled with pond water, causing her to stop swimming for a moment and cough. She was getting more tired by the second, but she did not dare to rest. She had already caused too much noise in this cold, wet, foreign environment where she was so helpless. And so she doubled her efforts, kicking the water with her feet, slapping it with her strong wings, to reach shore.

In the darkness below, the turtle now saw her. His eyes were weak, but she was an easy target, and that was exactly as he saw her, above him on the surface of the pond. She was a fluttering, flapping bull's-eye in the center of rings caused by her activity. Up he swam.

His great hooked jaws opened wide and snapped, causing schools of silver bubbles to churn around him. But the great jaws found only air, for just as he snapped the bat and her infant flopped out of the water and onto a flat rock, which the turtle could not easily reach. He lunged upward again and again, the claws of his feet trying for a footing which the slime of the rock did not afford. He could smell the warm, torturous fragrance of fresh food, and his beak opened to expose his yellow throat as he hissed his frustration at what, moments earlier, had been his prey.

With one last try he lunged up through the water, his body half-exposed, showing the great corn-colored half-moon of his undershell. For a second, he balanced on the edge of the rock; had he fallen forward, his beak would have cut into the bats as they lay exhausted and helpless on the rock's algae-green surface. But this was a kill the snapping turtle would not make. Falling backward into the pond with a loud *kerplunk*, he abandoned his pursuit, sinking deep into the dark water to the muddy floor. Opening his great hooked beak for one last time, he blew out a rage of tiny silver bubbles that frolicked back up to the surface as if in a happy, early-morning race.

For several minutes the black bat lay on the rock in a pool of muddy water. Wet and dirty, she was too spent to urge her wings to flight. She was still hungry, and with day now dawning, her infant would feel the stab of hunger and demand to nurse. With a valiant effort, up, up, up

she flew in an undisciplined melody of flight that bore her and her son away from the pond and over the willow tree.

Down below, the brown beetle moved unseen along the brown earth. Detecting another grub, he pursued it in haste, not staying in the safety of the shadows, but darting across a tiny patch of dawn. It was the beetle's first mistake of the morning, and it would be the last of his life. The mother bat danced down through the soft gray-gold of April. The kill was clean, the death swift. As her jaws closed on his head, he died without pain.

Entering the toolshed behind the house, the bat headed for her favorite rafter. Before roosting, she did a common but amazing stunt—a back flip in the air, so that she caught the splintered rafter's edge in an upside-down position. Here she would hang all day, until twilight, when hunger would again send her on her evening flight.

Folding her double-membrane wings about her, she held the dead beetle with her wingspur thumbs and ate it. Side to side and up and down, her rotary jaws crunched even the tough shell, forcing all the sweet and nourishing pulp into her gullet with a series of pronounced swallows.

Normally she ate and drank in flight, but the burden of her offspring tired her, and it felt good just to hang and rest. As she finished the beetle, her offspring slid down to the true nursing nipples at her breast. He bit sharply, aware not of her pain, but only of the pleasure he sought. There he sucked furiously until he could gulp his mother's warm, rich milk. Squirming with pleasure, he nursed himself full.

She closed her small, black eyes as he fed. He was her only offspring. In October, six months ago, she had mated. Her mate's sperm had rested dormant inside her all winter. A warm March day had activated it. After six weeks' gestation, her one male offspring had been born in that very toolshed.

Her wingspan was now fourteen inches. She was seven years old and had produced one infant every spring since her maturing. This was the sixth. It was almost May— he had come into the world rather early. All her others had been born in June.

The heat from the sun now shone directly on the toolshed. Inside, the warmth was welcome, as it helped to cure the early wetting in the pond. The young bat finished his nursing and resumed his hold on the false groin nipples. He fastened his sharp milkteeth into the almost nerveless tissue and slept.

Not his mother. Now that dawn had helped to dry her, she began one of her most carefully observed rituals.

Head to toe, she cleaned herself thoroughly, grooming her long, silky fur into a meticulous softness. Such was its thickness that her lighter-colored underfur had stayed dry during her unexpected dunking in the pond.

Wading ashore had muddied her feet, which nature had placed backwards on her body. There was mud between her toes to be removed. Pesky stuff. Using her long and sharp incisor teeth, she scraped away all traces of pond mud.

Clean at last! Nothing like a bath before bedtime. Unlike most of the human animals of the world, she was so clean that she was now completely free of body lice. Her fastidious toilet complete, her heartbeat decreased to almost a stop. Her squeaks subsided from thirty to ten per second. Her breathing reduced itself to about one percent of her oxygen intake in flight. In fact, she stopped breathing for eight whole minutes before she wrapped her wings more tightly about herself and her infant. In his sleep, he snuggled warmly against her and she felt the sweetapple fragrance of his nearness.

Then she slept.

Two

The April sun rose higher.

It warmed not only the belfry of the toolshed where the mother bat slept, cuddled with her son, but also the earth beneath.

Near one corner of the shed, an eight-inch hole was quite properly hidden in the tall grass. There was no loose dirt outside the hole, because it had been made from underneath. It was one of many that led to long inclined tunnels, ending at a cozy deep-earth burrow.

Inside, a marmot opened his bright, black, inquiring eyes, twitched his nose several times, and yawned. He was at once aware of a bothersome itch on his belly. Burying sharp incisor teeth into his white fur underside, he ended the itch (and it's maker, a tiny tick) with a tattoo of rapid nibbles. His long, graceful incisors were useful indeed, as he had no canine teeth. There was only a large gap between incisors and back molars which were his grinders.

Just to make sure the annoying itch would not return, the marmot scratched his belly with the four extended claws of his paw. His thumb, placed too high up on his foreleg to be of much use, did not come into play. Nor did he use the five toes on his hind foot, which jiggled as he scratched. With a quick decision, he ambled his stout, furry body up through the tunnel, poking his pink nose out from under the toolshed into the sunlight.

All clear.

He emerged into the daylight and felt the sun seep into

his partly gray, partly black, partly blond, partly brown fur. He was a pinto marmot. Two generations back, his grandmother had been an albino woodchuck. His mother had mated with a gray, and after a month, he came into the world. A year had passed since his birth, among a litter of five blind, furless, helpless kits. After four weeks, he had left his mother and had gone out on his own.

His first winter had been uneventful, as he spent the last four months of his first year sound asleep. But now it was April, and morning, and the sun was bright.

Instead of staying snug in his hole, he ventured forth, answering a stronger call than safety. The horn of mating had sounded and he would answer its call.

It was time he lured a female back to his hermitage, even if it meant fighting another male for her. This he was willing to do, and his fur would be torn many times in the pursuit of love.

Moving through the timothy grass, he inspected the green mound of a daisy plant. Too early. No tender flower stems were shooting up yet. The marmot liked daisies and buttercups, too. Oh, well. He ate a few of the early leaves, pruning the daisy plant back to almost ground level. Spying some early clover, he bounded over to it, and gobbled down his favorite food.

Off he waddled, up and across the lawn, down the hill, under a fence, stopping in a small grove of maple trees. Being so far from home, perhaps it was best to take a look around. It was getting too light to stay out of his burrow for a long time.

Using his sharp claws, he slowly climbed one of the maples—the first tree he had ever climbed, and certainly an indication of his maturity. As a kit, he would have been far less anxious to leave the nearness of earth, knowing full well that his avenue of escape from danger was directly down, not treeward. The marmot climbed higher. He paused several times for a chew on some maple buds. Early leaves were out, and their green and juicy stems were delicious. A nest of inchworms made his breakfast quite complete.

From a height of thirty feet in the maple tree he observed his toolshed. A man and a boy came out of the house and walked toward it. The marmot watched to see if they discovered his hole. They did not. It would have been a bother to dig or find another burrow during a season of courtship.

Down the maple he climbed, pausing only to take a refreshing sip from a sap bucket. Then he jumped the last two feet to the ground, landing in time to confront a small, but very curious, brown and white dog. Both animals were surprised at their meeting. The marmot bristled

the hair on his body to make himself appear bigger and more ferocious than his nine pounds.

The terrier was not a mature dog, and only half his adult size. His ears snapped erect. Twice they relaxed, as he wagged his tail. Ears straight up again, he barked three times. Was this marmot an enemy or a playmate? Happily, the terrier bounded forward, ready for a romp. But the woodchuck was not in the mood for games, especially with an adolescent dog—a future enemy, a digger of holes and an invader of snug, underground homes. As the dog landed on him, he gave the terrier a stout nip on the ear with his front incisors. The terrier yelped in pain and amazement, beating a retreat, and the woodchuck rambled off in the opposite direction, unhurried but annoyed that the terrier had delayed more pressing matters.

Only two houses away, a giant oak tree parasolled another backyard. At its base, the male marmot saw a tunnel entrance, and from it came the most enticing, the most exciting smell he had ever smelled.

Poking his snout inside the savory darkness, he did something he had never done before, and would rarely do in his lifetime. Tightening his lips, he blew a long, melodious trill. As its echo died deep down inside the burrow, he heard a faint but positive answering whistle.

Wasting not a second more, down into her tunnel he scrambled to a depth of six feet. As he descended, the pupils of his black beady eyes widened to compensate for the darkness. In his breast, his heart pounded as it had never pounded—not even when he had confronted the terrier. His teeth chattered.

At last he saw her. She was larger than he, at least

three or four pounds his senior. She was soft and beautiful. But she was not yet his. Nor was she to be won easily. As he advanced, her teeth bared into a menacing snarl that gave him pause. He pleaded with her, making a lyrical whine very softly from deep in his throat.

Showing off his coat, he rolled over in the leaves, coming to his feet again to face her. There could be no doubt that she was impressed with his grace and beauty. His throat caroled more of its love song, barely audible, but rising in pitch. A strange, new pulsation seemed to control his body. He quivered.

Slowly, ever so slowly, she lowered her head, letting the short, white fur under her chin touch the leafy floor of her burrow. He had never seen the gesture before, nor performed it himself, but he knew its meaning. It was her signal of willingness. She was his, and she would follow him home to his burrow. They would mate, hunt together, search each other's fur for ticks, and whistle back and forth their unmistakable mating tune.

A month later, five furless, helpless and blind little marmot kits began their lives in the warm darkness under the toolshed.

Three

Near the toolshed, a tool was being used.

The toolshed was surrounded by lawn grass, parted by a path and its delta at the door. In this hard, packed earth, a wasp was building her nest. Using her body as a battering ram, she penetrated the crust. Her front feet pawing the earth much like a tiny dog burying a tiny bone.

She paused in her digging to carry the loose dirt away from the entrance. She would permit no fresh dirt to betray the whereabouts of her nest. Pebble by pebble, she carried her debris from the hole into nearby deep grass, depositing each grain in a different spot.

One pebble she kept. This she used as a tool, a hammer with which she sculpted the entrance of the nest to her liking. Again and again she lifted the tiny stone high and smashed it into the mud. Blow by blow, the front door of her new home changed shape, barely large enough now to allow her passage.

And why not such perfection? After all, it was not just a humble nest. This was a palace, and the wasp was a queen.

Deeper and deeper she dug her living quarters, making room to store food, build honeycombs, lay and hatch eggs. Every morsel of dirt was carried up the tunnel, outside, and well away from the royal gate. She worked for ten hours without stopping. And only when her underground castle was complete did she stop to rest.

The nearby grass was timothy grass, tall and strong. High above the place where the queen had thrown her discarded diggings, a gray spider had built a web. Like the queen's palace, it too was a masterpiece of architecture. Its diameter was four feet, coming up from the ground, affixing its uppermost strands to the lower branches of two young alder trees.

The web was only three days old. Three days ago, the gray spider had climbed one of the alders, but there had been no wind, and so the spider waited in the alder tree until the next morning.

When it felt a breeze, it expelled the first long thread. The wind swept it into its current. But seconds later, the thread attached itself to the other alder, four feet away. The gray spider pulled its tent-rope tight, anchoring it in place by a tiny disc. The anchor disc was also a secretion from the spider's body.

Inch by inch, and belly up, the gray spider made the first trip underneath this horizontal tightrope. The strand bent only slightly with the weight. It was strong and smooth, since it was a travel route, not one of entrapment.

Had it been intended for snaring victims, the strand would have been sticky.

Strand by strand, the outer lines of the web were formed. Next came the radial lines, stretching from the center of the web to the outer frame. Struts were added, around and around, connecting the radial lines. These were not smooth and dull, but sticky and shiny to snare food. As a seamstress completes a dress, cutting away the unnecessary scrap, so the spider trims its web. The gray spider made a first inspection, passing from one face of the web to the other through the open port at the web's exact center.

Down the spider walked, along one of the lines to a hiding place near the foot of one of the alders. There the spider found a dead housefly, which was ignored, since this spider (like all of its kind) was not a scavenger. It preferred to kill.

Meanwhile, her majesty the wasp queen was ready. Extending her wings, she buzzed upward, starting on her first nuptial flight. The palace was ready. All it lacked was a mate, a royal consort, a male to become king of a whole new bloodline. So off she flew, into the web of the gray spider.

It was the wasp queen's first experience in a spider web. She charged the web, beating her wings against it in rage, but she succeeded only in binding herself tighter. As she saw the spider coming toward her, she buzzed a furious warning to keep away.

At the first impact, the gray spider ran upward along a transportation line, approaching the writhing wasp with caution. Early in its life, the spider had captured smaller

wasps, bitten into them, and found them unappetizing. These small wasps the spider merely killed and discarded, though not before once receiving a sickening sting. But the wasp queen was of good size, and from her thrashing, the gray spider knew she was far from dead. So carefully avoiding the wasp by several inches, the spider began to set the victim free. One by one, the spider cut the web strands that held the wasp. Off she flew, remnants of the broken web trailing behind her. The gray spider repaired the web and waited.

Until this point in time, the gray spider had been neither male nor female, but by the following day, its outer skin grew very hard. Internal glands then secreted a juice that loosened the spider's shell. Straining hard, the spider crawled out of it—body first, then legs—remaining inactive until the soft new skin stretched larger, and hardened into armor. Earlier it had lost a leg, but the new molting produced a bud which eventually became a new leg. This was the last and final molting. Only now were the gray spider's sex organs complete and mature. She was a large mare, and inside her, eggs were already forming.

The next visitor to her nest was a male gray spider, smaller than she, who mated with her. But before the eggs hatched into spiderlets, the male became listless. He lost interest in mating, even in eating. He was now a source of food, and he offered himself as food to the female, numb to the painless oblivion of death. She devoured him slowly and thoroughly.

In a matter of days, the gray spider's eggs hatched into spiderlets, which crawled off to begin lives of their own. A week later, their mother was eaten by a young male bat. He flew into the web, destroying both web and occupant in less than a second.

Several of the gray spider's offspring were later eaten by the wasp queen. The spiders were not killed at once. They were pounced upon, paralyzed with a sting, and dragged one by one into the palace. There they were kept fresh and stored for later use.

The wasp had mated too. She hunted and grazed with her mate, finding both meat and vegetation enjoyable. Often they munched on freshwater sponges that lived in the tiny stream that drained the toolshed.

Four

High in the willow tree, the flicker woodpecker stretched his wings but did not fly. He bobbed on his branch, showing the world the great white puff of his tail.

It was mid-morning. A man and a boy were walking back toward the house, carrying a saw from the toolshed. The flicker watched them intently until they passed. Then a new movement caught his eye. It was another flicker, a hen. She was at the foot of the willow, poking among the damp leaves with her bill, looking for grubs.

Hardly a twig on the willow moved as he left his perch, diving almost vertically to the ground, chirping his arrival. The hen pretended not to notice, continuing to poke under leaves. The cock walked around her, the feathers of his throat at full ruffle. The scarf of his plumage seemed redder, as if it were afire.

The hen noticed him, her throat clucking softly. Back and forth he marched before her, strutting to hold her attention. As he paraded to and fro, she began to face him directly, turning as he turned. They faced each other, less than two feet apart, re-enacting the ritual of the flicker courtship dance.

Using their beaks as wands, the cock and hen formed one U after another. Each semi-circular loop of the bill was accompanied by a bobbing of the body. Barely audible was a soft cooing noise, made only by the female.

The cock flicker won his hen. It took them three weeks to make a nest. It was started on a low branch by the

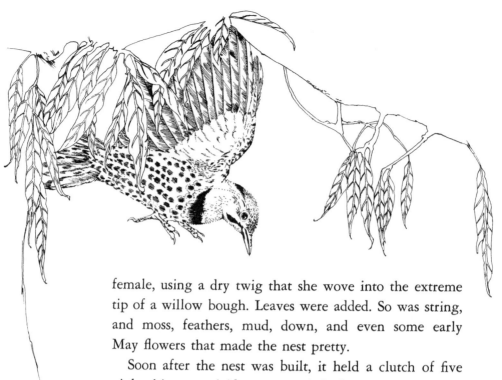

female, using a dry twig that she wove into the extreme tip of a willow bough. Leaves were added. So was string, and moss, feathers, mud, down, and even some early May flowers that made the nest pretty.

Soon after the nest was built, it held a clutch of five pink-white eggs, laid over a period of several days. They were often left unguarded as the weather was still a bit cold, and the hen had not yet decided to hatch them. They were inert. During this brief waiting period, hen and cock flew together looking for inchworms.

The wind had come. It blew over an aging elm, the top branches of which crashed into a low fork of the willow tree. There the elm stayed, on an incline, running from the crotch of the willow down to the ground. When the elm blew over at dusk, the flickers were not yet back at their nest, having been delayed by the storm.

In the torn earth at the elm's base was a hole. From this lodging appeared a pair of black, beady eyes and the black tip of a curious nose. He smelled his own earlier droppings, scats full of insect shells and winter seed.

Inch by inch, the skunk came out. He was surprised at the sudden demise of the elm under which he kept his burrow. Only surprised, not annoyed. The skunk was not easily excited. He was mature, and his complete calm was the serenity of skunkdom. But beware the chap who seems to have no temper.

He was not a tree climber; yet here was his chance—an elm that was so inclined. Up the trunk he strolled, tail straight up like a happy cat, wondering what sport he would find in the willow tree. It was spring and he was still drowsy from the long winter of reduced activity. His winter had been spent in an abandoned woodchuck burrow, along with several other skunks. It had been vacated by its former owner, a female marmot, due to an unusual and noxious smell, emitted by the skunk. The woodchuck had first thought of doing battle, and had even squared off against this casual black and white intruder. The skunk did not panic, nor did he fire more scent, but deep in his throat, he gave a low, catlike growl. It was a warning, the female marmot decided, to be heeded. The marmot sought newer, more fragrant quarters, rather than confront a weapon so strong its scent could carry almost half a mile.

Where the old elm met the willow, the skunk stopped. The branches were small now, telling him that he had gone far enough. Just as he turned to go earthward, he spotted the flicker nest and smelled its fresh contents.

Bird's eggs! Placing his round front paws (unlike his footshaped rear ones) on the edge of the nest, the skunk began to pry up one egg with his nose. Up he rolled it toward the edge of the nest. It fell back, cracked, and the skunk licked up its milky goodness.

As the skunk was about to repeat the treatment on the four remaining eggs, he heard a swift whirr of wings. Over his shoulder he saw a pair of yellow eyes moving toward him like two new moons, led by twin sets of open claws. He bolted, and luckily so. Huge talons bit deep into decaying elm bark as the rush of the great horned owl raked the tree. The owl screamed, hoping to paralyze the skunk into motionless fear.

But the skunk was not idle or cowardly. Twisting his body into a U-shape, he faced his attacker with both nose and rear. His head lowered, his hindquarters raised, he aimed and fired. The twin anal glands at the base of his tail loosed their overwhelming defense. Any animal or bird or man would have fallen from the elm at the instant of release, such was its unpleasant intensity. A drop of skunk scent on skin burns like acid.

And yet the firing of the skunk did not stop the great

horned owl. He was vicious with hunger; his gut ached with emptiness. Pulling his talons from where they had buried deep into the elm bark, the owl again rushed the skunk. Claws spread as double spearheads, he tried to ram the skunk from his precarious perch near the crotch of the willow tree, determined to sink his talons deep into the black and white fur to pierce the heart.

The next rush of the great horned owl proved helpful to the skunk, because the owl entangled his talons in a thatch of long, dangling willow strands that hung from the willow tree like hair. This provided the instant of delay that the skunk needed. Down the inclined trunk of the fallen elm he scampered, diving into the dark of his ground hole, where he was safe and relatively unharmed.

As it was, one of the owl's talons did rake the skunk, clipping off toes from the skunk's left hind leg. When the man and boy came out of the house after the storm to examine the fallen elm, there were traces of a struggle. Several feathers had fallen to the ground, from the owl's entrapment in the willow garlands. Along the inclined elm trunk was a dark trail of blood, made from the stump of the skunk's torn foot.

Meanwhile, the flickers had returned to their nest and were busily scolding the man and boy from their willow tree. Finding one egg of the original five smashed and eaten intensified their ire.

The boy held the lantern, and its soft ring of light did not include the flickers in its circle. He picked up several of the great horned owl's tailfeathers before he and his father returned to the house. The flickers settled down in their nest. The owl was now a quarter of a mile away, making a low but silent pass over the pond, hoping to spot a lily pad that cradled a sleepy frog.

Deep in the earth underneath the fallen elm, the skunk rejoined his family. Nuzzling his black and white mate, whose teeth chattered like a collie's at his homecoming, he curled up in a nook in the burrow, licking his wounded foot. When a treed skunk escapes a great horned owl, he is fortunate to lose only four flicker eggs, a few drops of blood, and a toe or two.

Later he would venture outside once again, this time to look for crickets, grasshoppers, beetles or earthworms, or to chew on the sweet timothy that grew near the tool-shed, or to look for snails in the tiny stream where the sponges were. As for now, it was enough just to be home and snug.

Licking his foot, he watched his mate trying to nurse their eight offspring. It was a large litter. A year ago she had only produced four. The eight skunk kits had been born three weeks ago, blind, pink, and defenseless. But even at birth their pink skin previewed the faint outlines of what would later be sharply defined black and white stripes. Now, at three weeks, eight pairs of black eyes were open.

In another month, at the age of seven or eight weeks, they would leave the burrow and hunt with their mother. Across the lawn, between the toolshed and the house, there would be nine skunks in single file—a small, soft, black and white chorus line, tails all erect, parading in the moonlight.

Five

The brown and white terrier pup was spending his first night outdoors.

May had turned warm, and the dog had been somewhat restless just before first light. His usual sleeping spot was the foot of the boy's bed, but tonight he was outdoors, to romp and prowl and bay at will. For several hours he had rested well on the old rug on the kitchen porch. Before dawn he was awake, stretching, and anxious for day.

Trotting across the back lawn he examined the strange position of the fallen elm. Any change warrants examination, and he sniffed at the freshly torn earth at its base. While emptying his bladder, his nose told him of the skunks' den. Despite an aura of unpleasantness, the dog walked closer, inserting his muzzle into the mouth of the burrow. He could smell life, the warm fresh blood of earthy creatures. With his front paws he attacked the entrance for several minutes, sending out small but rapid freckles of dirt around him.

He paused to see how his tailoring of the skunk hole now fit his shoulders. Still too narrow. But before he resumed the activity that made him a terrier, another motion distracted him. Over by the toolshed, the early feathering tops of the timothy grass moved with an abrupt rustle. At once the dog flattened, belly to ground. He inched forward, staying low. The nostrils of his black nose widened with each breath, straining for a scent. No clue. The cause of the rustle in the timothy grass, perhaps because of his extreme cleanliness, made no odor.

Silently now, and almost without effort, the blacksnake floated through the timothy. His last strike had hit a meal. His jaws had closed upon it, worked their way around it, engulfed it, and forced it back into his gullet. The acids of his belly were already rushing to meet, kill and digest it. Only then would his internal fluids hush their cry for an hour or two, and then he would again know hunger. Deep inside, his prey kicked the walls of his throat with vain attempts at escape. It even gave a last desperate squeal, heard several yards away by the dog.

The terrier froze as the blacksnake came out of the timothy, working his way across the lawn. Without knowing it, the blacksnake slid directly toward the dog. Closer now, the snake lifted his head. The young terrier, not quite knowing what else to do, jumped to his feet and gave a loud bark. Jerking back its oval head, the snake cocked itself into a coil position.

The dog leaped into the air, wanting neither to attack nor to retreat. The blacksnake made the decision. It turned, racing for the cover of high grass. The bounding terrier followed, his courage strengthened by the role of pursuer. With a delicate touch of his jaws, he gently nipped at the blacksnake's whipping tail, lifting the lower half of its body.

Perhaps to execute a faster escape, the blacksnake disgorged its kill, a small gray and white fieldmouse.

Inside the snake, the mouse had struggled for her life. The snake's gullet was dark and constricting, and without air. Already the warm digestive juices sought to dissolve her. The coma had almost begun, making her insensitive to pain and death, when the snake spat her out. Over she rolled, into the tall grass, rapidly regaining her awareness. Alert now, her body went rigid, ears up, eyes bulged, her long tail twitching in anxiety.

She was free. The dog was off somewhere chasing the blacksnake. With a last squeal of terror, the fieldmouse dove into the patch of timothy. A minute later she would no longer remember snake or dog. She busied herself with other matters. Stopping, she scratched away a troublesome tick behind her ear. She sneezed. Then using her nose to greater profit, applied it to the mouse trail and easily found her way home.

Earlier that evening she had heard the beating of huge wings, as a great horned owl had flown over her on his way to more filling prey. That too was forever forgotten. Had she been able to remember the many close calls of mousehood, as well as knowing that every weasel, rat, hawk, owl, and cat in the vicinity was stalking her, peace of mind would have been impossible. But the mouse now found herself completely unconcerned. Gnawing an alder root just for fun, she shortened her front incisor teeth. When they grew too long, as they constantly did, they prevented her from eating.

Back in her nest of soft hair and grass, she was greeted by her litter of young mice. Only three weeks ago she had mated. Her mate had fawned over her, and even helped her to build the nest. But after he contributed his sperm to her body, his function had been served. With nips, claws, bites, and a series of irate squeaks, she drove him away.

When her brood of six became mature and left her, she would mate again. Finding another mate would be easy. The patch of timothy grass sheltered several thousand mice. So many, in fact, that they caused a food shortage, a space shortage. She often lacked the isolation from all others that females with young crave.

She lay on her side as her offspring sought the teats and the warm mouse milk. Feeling them nurse, she nibbled an oat seed.

She was still hungry, but she had eaten the last seed. As she rose to her feet, her litter held fast. They too were hungry, and would not be ready for even a momentary weaning until they were three weeks old. She moved about

the nest. They clung to her, still nursing with a barely audible *suck, suck, suck*. Had she run from the nest, pursued by an attacker, their six mouths would have held fast, riding with her and nursing blithly through it all. Such was their hunger, and hers. Her instinctive answer to this population-food balance problem was swift. Using her sharp incisor teeth, she killed three of her litter. It was the only thing to do, and she did it. She was only a tiny gray and white mouse, but the sacrifice of half her litter was a sign of her responsibility to all life.

Before firstlight, a predator came calling. But this time it was not the blacksnake. Tasting the air with his nose, he stalked closer and closer to her nest. As he approached, the mouse could hear his footstep rustling the dry timothy. Waiting for him, her body became rigid with fright. He was closer now, so close that she could even detect his smell—a sharp, strong scent that hurt her delicate nose and made her eyes blink.

Beneath her belly, her three remaining offspring finished nursing and squirmed against her, competing for the comfort of her warmth. She wanted to run, knowing that she could probably elude him in the maze of narrow mouse-tunnel patterns that she and other mice had built into the close weave of timothy grass. There was no stopping him. On he came, and she could see him now—a large and hungry male skunk, with black, beady eyes and a twitching black nose that sought her and her brood.

Suddenly he froze, looking directly at her. Just as his open snout stabbed through the thin veil of timothy, she bolted, diving through the matting of grass that would be her shield. The skunk did not follow at once, busying himself with eating the three remaining baby mice in her nest. Giving up his search for her, he left as quietly as he had come.

Alone in the night, her small body remained stone still for several minutes, allowing her tiny heart to quiet its beating and her series of rapid pants to become less frequent. Then she calmly returned to her den, and curled up in a soft, round gray and white ball, to sleep in peace.

Come evening, she would mate.

Six

Up near the crotch of the willow tree, the four flicker eggs had hatched into birdlets. The hen stayed close to her brood. The cock kept busy feeding his family from dawn to twilight.

This morning he was awakened somewhat earlier by the barking of the brown and white terrier. Opening his eyes, he shifted his perch on the twig near the edge of the nest. The branch moved slightly. Inside the nest, the four birdlets felt the sway, but remained unconcerned. Early in life, they had begun to read the movement of their nest. When a parent departed, the nesting branch twitched a certain way. This meant no food. But when the parent returned, it produced a different jolt. This meant food, and four mouths yawned wide, exposing their pink, hungry throats.

So when the flicker cock left his twig that morning, they did not stir. The cock glided over the toolshed, landing on the lower end of the fallen elm. He pruned a wing feather, and billed down his freckled breast. This done, he flew to one of the alders just past the toolshed.

Spotting prey, the dark of his eyes grew deeper as he concentrated on the slug snail. The alder, however, was wet with dew. Footing was unsure, making the rapier thrust of the flicker's bill go off its mark.

The snail reacted. Coiling into a ball, it dropped from the alder into the timothy. There it remained stone still. The flicker cock went after it. In its ball shape, the snail

rolled down through a gap in the thick floormat of timothy. After a brief search, the flicker abandoned it.

The slug snail stayed balled for almost ten minutes. Unlike box snails, it had no shell into which it could retreat. The stab of the flicker's bill had cut off one of its extended eyes, but that was no loss. Another would grow.

The snail unfolded. It moved up through the grass on its single foot, its underside rippling less than once a second. Up another alder tree it climbed, leaving behind it a mucus path, shiny in the May morning sun. The mucus on which it glided was a useful secretion, acting as a lubricant along an unsmooth route. Like the spider in a nearby alder, the snail left a dragline of its own making wherever it went. If lost, it could retrace its course by backtracking along this dragline.

Once again the snail climbed the alder. The sun's warmth increased, causing the snail to move to the shady side of the trunk as it worked its way out along a lower branch. Not finding the grazing it sought, it began to leave the underside of the alder branch and drop slowly, slowly into space. It was descending by its dragline, inch by inch. A wind gust made the gray spider move in her web. The snail reversed direction, climbing back up its thread to the alder branch.

Sometime back, the snail had been a male. It had passed through a neuter stage of its life and was now a female. Farther out along the branch, she was surprised by another snail. This one was younger, but a mature male. Slowly, for this is the way snails do everything, he moved closer to her, until their faces met and touched. The snail had mated before, but as a male. As a female, she was virginal.

Twisting and squirming themselves together, they stroked one another again and again. It was not yet intercourse. That would not happen today.

A day later, the snails chose to mate. From their heads they each fired a dart into the other—male to female, female to male. This was not a genital exchange. The body exchange occurred elsewhere, as their vents joined.

The actual intercourse happened in mid-air. The snails were suspended from the alder by twin threads. Mating took place as they swung in the May breeze.

Afterward, a delicious dinner was enjoyed, composed of minute tree lice and alder leaves. The meal was not rushed. Each snail ate leisurely, chewing each bite thoroughly, with the help of 20,000 teeth-like grinders.

Later she left him for more important matters. Down by her threadline she drifted, entering the tall grass. Finding a hole in the dead brown matting, she molded a tiny nest in the black earth. Pausing not a moment upon completing the nursery, she laid a mass of tiny pearl-white eggs, about a dozen. She might have laid half or twice that many.

Three hours later, a young snail hatched. He was the first of the clutch to do so. Breaking from his egg crust, he was hungry, even though his outer body had not yet hardened into opacity. His appearance was watery. Regardless, the baby snail left the nest where his siblings still incubated, and which his dam had deserted. He made his way along the damp, dark earth. It was an exciting venture, and his tiny heart was beating almost eighty times a minute.

Another young male was nearby. A very young marmot. For the first time he peeked his black nose from the hole under the toolshed.

He saw the young snail and watched his tiny heart beat through his transparent body for several seconds. And ate him.

Seven

One hundred years ago, a fat brown acorn fell from a black oak.

For two years before that, the acorn had clung to a twig end, nestled in the pointed leaves. At first it was no more than a tiny bud. It had taken the warmth of two springs and two summers to expand it into maturity.

Slowly, its strong green umbilical stem dried and weakened to gray, eventually giving way when a late September wind whipped the twig that held it. It fell for almost one hundred feet, landing on a drumhead of matted oak leaves and moss with a final thump, giving a start to a gray squirrel only inches away.

But his fear was soon gone. He had heard acorns fall before and it was a welcome sound, now that winter was coming. Running to it, the gray squirrel picked up the acorn in his clever paws, twisted it to the correct position, and bit off its useless, pulpy-tasting cap to expose the round, yellow, soft "moon." Stuffing it into his mouth, he scampered off, rustling through year-old leaves toward his cache. Deciding, however, that his storehouse, already holding almost a thousand acorns and hickory nuts, was too far away to warrant a hauling and hoarding of just one more acorn, he buried it instead.

As winter hardened and his food supply drained, the squirrel would have returned to dig it up. But no such unearthing occurred. A redtail hawk, with a belly already empty from winter, ringed high in the air to scan hundreds of acres with his excellent sight and hearing, and the gray squirrel chose the wrong moment to cross open ground from a hickory to a swamp maple. Folding his wings tightly against his body, the hawk dropped silently, and his talons found the squirrel's throat and paunch.

But that was one hundred years ago. The buried acorn had long since sent its creamy sprout fingering into the earth, to grow with time into a great old oak tree.

The oak was so giant that its uppermost branches were unchallenged for sunlight; not even a neighboring tulip tree standing flagpole straight could overtower it. Near the oak's top, over the place where the marmot had first whistled to his mate, there was a nest—a thicket crown of twisted branches that cupped a basin of bark and dead leaves lined with the fur and bones of small animals and with feathers—the nest of the great horned owl.

It was hardly a cozy nook of comfort, but rather a command post of defiance—a place from which to defy the

wind, rain, and snow. Often he would bark that this territory was his, and his alone. Woe betide those who chal-
lenge his warning, except for a family of wrens who nested
nearby. For some reason, his august presence tolerated
these tiny birds to be near him even now, when his nest
held his mate and young. The wrens ate insects that he
found pesky, and they also danced through the lace of oak
leaves in much too quick a fashion for him to pursue them.
So the owl let the wrens remain.

Near his nest, the live oak branches were marked and
scarred, the bark rubbed clean where great talons paced
to and fro. Even the tough oak bark yielded to the crush
of those claws. So had a locally feared tomcat, who had
been so bold and unwise as to confront the owl, and
whose head had been torn from his buff-colored body in
seconds.

When the great horned owl had made his kill of the
large tomcat, he bore it to the top of the oak, his talons
buried deep in the warm flesh. At the nest, he held the
cat down with his feet, using his beak to tear meat from
his kill to share with his mate and their three offspring.
The three were growing steadily bigger, and steadily hun-
grier and more demanding. When he returned to the nest

with his talons empty, they often hissed their disdain for his failure as a hunter, sometimes even lunging at him to cut short his stay at home, prompting him to take wing again.

Thus the great horned owl hunted from before sunset until well after dawn. He hunted until his wings ached with fatigue and his searching eyes smarted with wanting to close and sleep. If the hunting was poor, he continued through the morning. Constant hunger also plagued his mate, and she often flew with him. Even though there were field mice aplenty, he alone had to catch and eat twenty for a meal. Bones and all, he ate them. Later, he orally disgorged the undigestable bones, skulls, fur and feet, expelling them as pellets of waste.

Behind the toolshed, the soft blanket of timothy sloped away toward the pond in the meadow. Daisy buds had opened their bright yellow cartwheels, and black-eyed Susans would soon follow. Some of the Susans were late to appear; these were baby plants, only pinhead in size, but each first leaf was already velveted with minute green-white fuzz. Discs of majestic Queen Anne's lace began to spot the meadow, each white circle a community of over a thousand tiny blooms. The grass was thick and strong, bending over obligingly to roll into a web of tunnels and runways.

Nibbling at a broad-leaf weed, the cottontail rabbit seemed totally devoted to the sweet green juices of her salad. The weed was cool and thirst-quenching, so much so that for an instant she closed her eyes to enjoy it. Her long ears alertly swept the area, her hearing and eyesight fanning in all directions without even a slight turn of her head.

Her nose, even as it sought more food, sipped the evening wind for telltale scents. Crunched down in the grass, she felt the bones of her shoulders almost touch behind her head. Her body was relaxed, yet in a second it could become rigid in its total clench for escape, if escape was called for. She knew her meadow was rife with foes. Across the pond there were marsh hawks and owls. Weasels and stoats were aplenty, even in the very earth where she had her burrow. Blacksnakes were also to be reckoned with, not for cottontail rabbits her size, but for her young. Only a few hours ago she had been chased by a brown and white terrier and a cat. Yet she enjoyed the leaf that nourished her, its juices answering both her hunger and her thirst.

Spring felt good to her, and although it was evening, she knew its warmth deep under her thick fur. Winter had persisted long and hard, the snow had been deep. Several times she had been unable to wade through the drifts, strayed too far from her burrow, and had almost died of exposure. She had gone without food during one blizzard, chewing only on the black twigs that whiskered up between the drifts. So the spring was welcome, for had it come only one week later, she would have perished under the snow—a common death among rabbits.

Chewing the last of the broad leaf, she felt a renewed sensation, of new life kicking impatiently inside her swollen belly. Exactly one month ago, this doe cottontail had mated with a buck slightly larger than she. He had

mounted her often, and after the four or five violent and rapid thrusts ended, he was both playful and proud with her. Of all this love and harmony she had little or no recall. A week ago she had become aloof; she stopped letting him have her or be near her. She avoided his company, and even the companionship of other females or juveniles. Yet he kept coming around, imploring her to accept him. But after one particularly vicious kick that she landed on his soft seeking nose, the buck left her and did not return.

Back in her nest, fighting the increasing torment of her contracting uterus, her eyes seemed to pop from her temples. Eventually her labor rewarded her with four small fawns. Breathing hard, and wet with the work of it, she rested only a moment before licking them thoroughly, rump to head, with her delicate tongue. They were blind and helpless and naked, and in color neither pink nor blue, but a sullen sunset of inbetween. She continued washing them with her mouth and tongue until they responded to the mothering enough to nurse. As they nuzzled her, her eyes closed in contentment, feeling their soft noses search her belly fur for milk, find it, and tug at her with the fire to survive. In the morning, she jumped from the nest to establish her watch. Before leaving, she touched each of the four fawns with her nose, covering her nest with a roof worked from weeds and tripgrass, with its lightly scented lavender blooms that were also neither quite pink nor blue.

During the next few days, the cottontail rabbit doe never paid call to her young except during the dark of night. Daylight hours were spent standing sentry a short distance away. Her fawns were only hours old when the brown and white terrier came thrashing through the timothy. At the first sniff of her litter he turned toward the nest, and this was the exact moment the doe had waited for. Bounding from her watch, she ran directly at him, darted quickly to one side; and then once she had him pursuing her, let him chase her away from the nest.

Several times as he stalked her, she froze in the open meadow and was stone still waiting for him. Confident of

her own zigzag speed, she knew she could outrun anything that chased her, especially a half-grown terrier who lacked reason as much as poise. Outrun him she could, but just in case, in her mind was a pattern of escape holes she had put to memory. Her sharp instinct told her which hole was nearest even though she could not see it, and it would be to this very hole she would dart if the dog got too near. Farther and farther from the nest she led him, until she felt that her nursery and its squirming scramble of young rabbits was secure.

In a day or two, the hairless, wormlike babes changed into soft, furry balls of constant activity. More and more they looked like the doe, although their eyes were still shut and they were quite deaf. As soon as the darkness deepened, the cottontail left her watch. Feeling the fawns tenderly with her feet, she stepped gracefully into her nest and nursed them, letting them romp over her in their blind search for warmth, food and love. In only two weeks they would mature enough to flee their hideout, leaving their mother forever. But now, she could feel them tumble about her, responding so completely to her nightly visits.

The two weeks passed. The litter of cottontail fawns matured, and independence day arrived. High in the sky, the night moon was white and full, lighting the outside world. Three of the fawns slipped quietly away and out into the night. Only one remained, staying close to the doe. She kicked him from the nest, but despite his surprise and hurt, he came back. Trying another ruse, the doe herself left the nest, knowing he would follow her. She ran across the meadow in a crazy, undisciplined pattern, often unseen in the runways of the timothy. The fawn tried to

equal her speed, but in only seconds she outdistanced him. On he ran, climbing an earth mound until he saw her once again, sitting still in the moonlight.

Such was his joy at seeing her that he bounded toward her without caution. Nearing her, he was only faintly aware of the whisper of giant wings over his head. Nor was he fully aware of the sharp hooks of the great horned owl that almost raked his small back.

The doe heard the wings, and saw the talons just as they buried into her flank. She tried to run, to kick, anything to heal the pain and fear of capture. But her struggle was short, ending in a futile death cry such as a wounded human child might make. It was the only noise she had ever made in her lifetime—one agonized note. Again the young rabbit heard the wings as the hungry hunter bore away his food. The young buck was alone in the meadow, seeing nothing but moonlight, feeling not a warm and loving mother's tongue caressing his fur, but instead a chilling and lonely night wind, and hearing only the intense beating of his small, frightened heart.

Minutes later his trembling stopped. His mother's death now forgotten, he hopped happily but quickly across the meadow, through the dogbane and into the timothy. He even bypassed his birthplace. Although the soft fur and grass that lined the nest still kept it warm, this, too, was not to be remembered. Nose twitching, he nibbled a mushroom cap and found it to his liking.

The white moon was obscured on and off by cloud puffs, each one getting bigger and blacker, coming from the west. Jagged cracks of ivory-colored lightning split the darkness as wars of thunder growled to overtake them, sounding before the lightning flashes faded. The storm closed the meadow, driving the young cottontail into the dry, deep earth, where he conquered his wetness and fear.

High in the oak nest of twisted branches, the warm meat of the cottontail doe was being torn into and fought over by the owl's mate and three offspring. Nearby, the great horned owl gripped his perch. As he watched them eat, he was smartly aware that his own belly was near empty and the hurt of it made him bark his envy. The blood on his claws was still red, still fresh, but the driving rain was hitting him now and washing away the marks of his kill. Legs spread wide, wings extended, he tried to beat back at the wind and rain. Beak open, he screamed his rage, defying the storm that delayed his hunting and sent his prey running underground. Again he screeched at the thunder and lightning, declaring himself master of his oak, crown of his kingdom, lord of his mandate.

He was master of all but his own hunger.

Eight

Come morning, the storm was over. The sun was up, shining on small crumbs of rabbit meat that lay in the grass under the oak.

By noon, the sun was hot. The meat crumbs had already started to decay. The brown and white terrier sniffed at them, taking too ambitious a whiff. The stench filled his nostrils and he moved on.

Not so the black ant. She and her kind were scavengers; to her, the decaying meat was a pungent invitation to feast. Her mandibles pinched into the meat, her strong jaws tore at it. Eating her fill, she left the meat crumbs, heading toward the nest of her colony, not far from the base of the willow tree.

The black ant carried nothing homeward to her anthill. She could not have lowered herself into the position of a worker ant. She was a scout, and though both scouts and workers were neuter-females, scouts were higher in the pecking order. It would have been beneath her dignity to make herself a porter of rotting meat.

Warrior ants at the entrance to the colony hill recognized her, allowing her to pass. Once inside and down the long main chute, she approached a waiting platoon of workers. To get their attention, she waved her antennae for several seconds. As an encore, she belched a minute portion of decayed rabbit. This was the clincher. The platoon of porters followed her back to the food source,

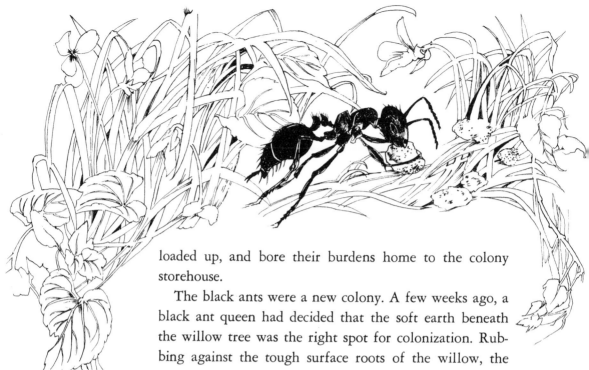

loaded up, and bore their burdens home to the colony
storehouse.

The black ants were a new colony. A few weeks ago, a
black ant queen had decided that the soft earth beneath
the willow tree was the right spot for colonization. Rub-
bing against the tough surface roots of the willow, the
queen purposely broke off her wings. Digging a hole in the
ground, she then laid her eggs. But only a few. She could
not lay more than she could guard and feed by herself.
(A few days earlier she had mated, her mate dying shortly
afterward.) Days later, this first modest clutch of eggs
hatched into neuter females. Their job would be to attend
and feed the queen.

Attended by her new servants, the ant queen was free
to produce more eggs. Some of the new clutch of eggs
were given extra-rich food. These eggs would hatch into
males and females. But the ant queen did not want more
queens about. Before they could hatch, pupate, fly off and
breed, she killed every potential queen. There would be
no rivals to her throne.

Not far from the willow was a small stand of young

white birch trees. It was in this direction that the scout who had found the decaying bits of rabbit was going. The trip from willow to birches took her over two hours. Not once did the black ant stop to rest.

Reaching the foot of a white birch that was no more than an inch in diameter, she began to climb its slightly twisted trunk. The first branch was four feet from the ground, and she crawled out along it. Reaching the end of the limb, she examined the face of a new leaf. She walked the underside, searching. The scout ant found what she sought—an aphid. Not a hard find, for the young white birches were full of them.

She came to the aphid slowly, not wanting to startle it. The aphid was aware of her presence, but it did not run or fly. Gently, the scout moved to the aphid, and using her antennae, made the first contact. The aphid jumped slightly, but did not bolt. Using great care, the ant began to softly caress the aphid. It responded to the stroking, producing a tiny drop of milky fluid. This the ant tasted and liked. The black ant gently lifted the aphid, using her strong mandibles. It did not squirm or attempt escape, as the scout tenderly carried her pet back to the colony near the base of the willow.

The trip from colony to birches and back had taken the ant almost all afternoon. But she did not quit, or even set down her burden, until she reached home, entered the

anthill, and presented the new aphid that she had already domesticated to her clan. Once again she caressed the aphid until it produced more specks of the milky material. Without hesitation another ant scooped it up and carried it off to the royal nursery.

Only then did the scout leave her pet aphid, to munch on part of a dead housefly that one of the workers had lugged home. This was followed by something sweeter for dessert, a bit of nectar.

Checking once more on her aphid to see that it was comfortable and bedded down snugly in its new quarters, the scout retired for the night. She sought her favorite sleeping nook, in a group of other scouts. She would not bed down among the worker females, as they were her inferiors. Working together for the colony's well-being was one thing—seeking their company during off hours was another.

After a very brief antennae-waving chat with another female, the black ant scout rested. It had been a long hunt, and a longer trek home with her prize.

Nine

Just this side of the pond, there was an open place. It was too far from the water for the tall marsh grass, too near for meadow grass such as clover. The soil was sandy. Here and there the dunes were spotted with small mounds of green, with long tines covering each—a desert dappled with green spikes of grass.

It was the perfect place for the snapping turtle to lay her eggs. Sometime ago, she and the big male of the pond had joined, mating in the water. After the mating, they went their separate ways, not bothering to keep company. Prior to their becoming mates she had seen the big snapping turtle rarely, although they had lived in the same pond for over twenty years. They met by accident.

Several weeks ago, the brown and white terrier had come to the pond. Despite his thrashing among the lilies in the shallow end, he finally managed to catch one of the big bullfrogs. Killing it with one bite, he became bored with it, leaving it in the water near some rocks.

Other than some water nymphs and mayflies, the female snapping turtle had been the first to find the dead frog. Tearing off large bites of the soft white meat with her beak, she was enjoying her feast of rotting flesh. As she fed, she was distracted by the presence of a rowbug. This tiny, inch-long backswimmer made his way past her huge snout, his two small oars sculling smartly along. Annoyed, she halfway snapped at him. But taking a gulp of air, he dived deep into the mud and leaves, eluding her.

It was then that larger competition for the bullfrog car-
cass came.

Great and magnificent jaws broke the water near where
she fed. He crawled from the black pond water, pouring
silver from his giant, jagged shell. His back was covered
with mud and slime. His beak opened wide to show the
great egg-yellow mouth. Seeing her, he hissed a warning.

Dropping the dead bullfrog, the female turtle moved
to avoid his charge. Blocking her every move, and her
every attempt to reach the water, he ignored the frog. The
splashing in the water washed it away. It floated belly-up,
ghost white in the moonlight.

The upper hooked jaw of the big snapper found a hold
on the female. He dragged her into the water with him
and there he mated with her, holding her tight against him
with his large clawed flippers.

Once again he mated with her, and then he was gone,
returned to the thick mud and bed of leaves at the pond's
bottom. She did not see him again.

The mating had passed. Now it was time for her to

leave the pond. It was just dark when she pulled herself from the water, her shell ringing twice as she stumbled across the wet, round shore stones. Up the bank she crawled, past the patch of marsh grass, to the place where the sand was soft. Choosing a spot that was not sheltered at all by tree leaves and would get the full sun of daylight, she started her nest.

Using her front flippers alternately, she began the arc near her nose, swinging her claw back toward her tail. The sand flew into the humps of dry grass. Digging until the basin in the sand was about half a foot deep, she was satisfied. One at a time, like pink-white golf balls from a weathered golfbag, she expelled the eggs from her. Nine times her body strained, each spasm producing a wet egg. After the ninth, she was tired. There were no more eggs inside her.

With her flippers she again made the sand fly, this time covering the cluster of white eggs. They were not soft like the eggs of wood turtles. These were snapper eggs, and already they were harder and tougher, much like the character of their parents. Gradually the sand covered the eggs, but the snapping turtle was not through. Her body stamped the sand down. She moved in circles, making sure that the sand was tightly packed around her clutch of eggs.

Her flat undershell completing its masonry in the sand, she left the dune area, crawling slowly back to the pond. Her brain had now forgotten about her eggs. If chance brought her again to the spot where she had deposited them, she would ignore them, passing over them without concern. Flopping into the pond with an exhausted *kerplunk*, she sank slowly to the dark mud at the bottom.

A blast of excess air in her lungs sent two columns of bubbles rising to the surface.

All this had happened over two months ago. June had come and gone. July brought its long, hot days. Down in the sand, the nine turtle eggs baked in the heat. The surface sand, ground smooth by the female turtle and again by wind and rain, formed a lid to the nest, holding the warmth tight against the eggs.

Hard though it was, the crust suddenly heaved upward in one small spot. It was not a big thrust. Only a few grains of dune sand tumbled from their floor pattern. Another thrust followed, and more. Each attack dislodged more sand, until he finally appeared. Poking his tiny curved snout into the late-afternoon sunlight, he took his first look at the world, and found it welcoming. Flapping all flippers, he spurted from the sand, hatched.

Although only the size of a silver dollar, he was an exact model of his sire, the giant snapping turtle. And like his sire, his two main desires were the dark seclusion of deep water, and food. Without pause, he pointed his tiny hook nose straight toward the pond (although he had never seen it, and could not see it now), and began his long journey to the fresh water that would be his home. The turtle made tiny tracks in the sand, as if a boy had taken a toy tractor, set it in the dune sand pointing toward the distant pond, and let it go.

Evening came cloudy, and the pond and its environs became silent and still. There was no wind, and even the many bugs of the dunes and meadow seemed to be more quiet and cautious.

Still crawling toward the pond, the young snapper was

tired. Yet he dragged himself forward, making a *runch*, *runch*, *runch* with his undershell as it scraped over the many pebbles in the dune sand crust. The great horned owl passed directly over the small turtle, but did not hear the sound.

But the noise of the turtle was heard by other ears. They were small, mean-looking ears that were almost entirely buried in the fur of their owner—ears set closely on a sharp gray face. Two ears that were intently aware of the sounds made by the tiny turtle.

Ten

Watching the young snapping turtle was a tiny pair of black beady eyes. The eyes were smaller than pinheads, and compared to the keen nose and alert ears of their owner, they were quite weak. But eyesight was his only weakness. Pound for pound, or rather ounce for ounce, no predator in the meadow attacked or killed as neatly as the shrew.

His small body began with a black nose at the tip of a snout so sharp it could almost pick a lock. The shrew's mouth was lined with long, needle-sharp, red-tipped teeth. The mouth was large, much too large for his minute size. His body was only two inches long, his weight less than half an ounce. The butt of his gray-brown body ended with a stubby, lighter-colored tail.

On his sharp face, eyes were almost non-existent. But his ears heard the scrape of the young turtle's belly shell along the dune sand, and his nose smelled the aroma of fresh turtle meat.

Unknowingly, the young turtle advanced directly toward the shrew. But suddenly he stopped, lifting his small head high in the air. He blinked. The distance between them was over eight feet, but the shrew ran it in less than a second. Before the young snapper could draw his head back into his shell, the shrew was upon him, directly under the hook of his jaw. The turtle opened his small mouth, trying to hook his already strong beak into his attacker.

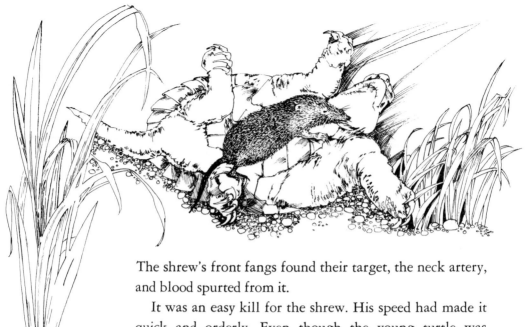

The shrew's front fangs found their target, the neck artery, and blood spurted from it.

It was an easy kill for the shrew. His speed had made it quick and orderly. Even though the young turtle was twice his size and triple his weight, there had not been much of a struggle. He had flipped the turtle over on his back, the yellow of the undershell shining in the dark sand. The claws and flippers of the turtle had raked him once or twice, tearing at his fur. But in three seconds it was over. The shrew had severed the artery, and the turtle retreated to the coma of death.

Had the turtle been twice the size, it would not have deterred the shrew. This was not the first turtle he had slaughtered. Two days ago, he had come across a small wood turtle among the alders. He had killed it in ten seconds. The newly hatched snapper offered even less resistance.

Breaking the spine and tearing off the head, the shrew began chewing the throat and tender windpipe. Pushing his snout into the shell as far as possible he ate the deliciously warm, soft internal organs. Leaving only the half-empty shell and claws behind, the shrew left his kill.

He moved across the dune sand in short, running bursts, stopping for several seconds. He was still hungry, and his metabolism was still high. His heart pumped over one thousand times and he breathed eight hundred times every minute. He slept often, sometimes for ten seconds, rarely as long as a minute. In the three hours following his leaving the turtle shell, the shrew ate an earthworm, a small tree frog, and a gray spider.

Come dawn, he was still active. Day and night made no difference to him, as he almost never slept for more than an hour. He was constantly plagued by his own ruthless appetite. He had been hungry since his birth in that same meadow, just below the toolshed, three months ago.

At birth he had been almost too small to see. His was one of a litter of four. Had the litter numbered one hundred, they would not have weighed even one full ounce together. Only days after he was born, blind, pink and helpless, he opened his eyes, grew hair, left the nest for good, and hunted.

Hunting was his main occupation, and with good cause. He ate three to four times his own weight each day, yet he was constantly hungry. Only just after he had filled himself on a fresh kill was he ever free of pain. Emptiness haunted him an hour later. Two hours, and he would be almost insane with hunger. In five or six hours without food he would starve.

Some of the timothy was going to seed. A sparrow flew from high in the willow tree, grounding herself in open meadow where the timothy seeds fell. She landed too near, where the shrew's sensitive nose could smell her flesh and almost feel her warmth.

He had been sleeping for twenty seconds—for him, a refreshing nap. His pace had retarded, pulse to six hundred, breath to five hundred per minute. But now he smelled sparrow, and was pleasantly awakened by the fragrance of breakfast. He could not see her, but he ran to her in short darting fits of speed that covered ground almost instantaneously. In less than a minute he was upon her. She had delayed her flight too long, and she would pay dearly for her carelessness.

There was the muffled sound of a missile hitting soft feathers. Hooking deep into her throat, his long incisors sought her artery. Being almost ten times his weight, she tried to fly, but could not. Rising only seven feet off the ground, she fluttered back to earth, dead by the time she hit. During her rise and fall, the shrew fanged her throat.

Feathers flew. Ripping open the dead bird, he gorged himself on the tender organs. He ate the breast meat and one of the legs. Bite by bite, the burning in his belly was calmed.

He had covered his white chest fur with gore in lunging at the innards. Carefully he cleaned himself, removing all traces of sparrow blood until he was immaculate. When his front was to his liking, he sneezed a tiny sneeze, spitting out a feather.

Closing his black beady eyes, the shrew slept soundly for almost five minutes.

Eleven

The pond where the giant snapping turtle lived was a small, round one, less than fifty yards across.

Cattails grew on one bank, and the shafts that supported what would look like furry brown hotdogs were now summer-thick. Around a curve in the pond, a cluster of water lilies floated. Their pads lay comfortable on the silver surface, connected by the endless wakes of waterbugs. One lily cradled a big blue dragonfly, shining iridescent in the morning sun.

Some feet away at the shoreline, a patch of arrowroot shook their triangular heads. Some of the arrowroot had flowered into white hyacinth, and the blooms were well buttoned with rows of green dots. Upshore, past the arrowroot, clumps of brackens feathered out strong and green.

The pond's bottom was a blend of muck and sand, quilted with layer upon layer of black leaves. Many of the leaves fell from the sassafras trees that seemed to thrive, as many of the laurel family do, near pond water. Behind the laurels, on higher ground, were maples, and alone on the peak of the rise, a lonely sweet gum.

Deep in the pond, where the water was black, the great snapping turtle was hungry. This was a fact that he kept to himself, making no noise at all to express his displeasure.

Among the quiet lily pads, a ripple began. The ring swelled outward into nothingness. At its center, a head

appeared. Two bulging eyes popped out. Below the mouth, a white throat bubble began to expand and contract, its muscular action pumping air in order to breathe.

Like the snapping turtle, the cow frog had been a resident of the pond for over twenty years. Apparently she was as wise as she was old and big, for in nature, only the wise and wary live that long.

Hanging on the edge of a large lily pad, she rested. Body in the water, she hung one webbed hind foot on a lily stem, waiting. Only inches away, on a neighboring pad, the blue dragonfly might come her way. His error would be costly. In this pond, first mistakes were often the last. Luckily for the dragonfly, the big cow frog did not wait that long. Only several seconds before he flitted to her lily pad with his uneven buzz, she slipped into the water, swimming away with whipping kicks from her powerful thighs.

Deeper in the water, her dark green color seemed almost black. Her body spurted ahead, gliding almost five feet per stroke. Again she surfaced among the reeds. Her head popped out farther this time, exposing the dots below her eyes. The dots were her ears, smaller than her eyes, showing that she was female.

The bullfrog who had mated with her had eardots larger than hers. His were even larger than his eyes. He had been a foot and a half long. Since their mating in the water, she had not seen him. Nor did she care. At the moment her body was heavy with over ten thousand eggs, perhaps even twice that many. The eggs made her large and slow. It was always this way. They also made her too restless to even wait for the blue dragonfly to approach close enough to snare.

It was time. Holding a reed shaft with her hand-like forelegs, her rump opened to expel (in about three good squirts) a gray, jelly-like mass of eggs—far more than ten thousand. Almost magnetically, the jelly mass found a reed shaft and encircled it. It was a sunny place, and the eggs would hatch into tadpoles in a matter of days. Each gray egg contained a minute black speck, and each speck would soon have a tiny tail.

Meanwhile, the cow frog was still hungry. Turning about, her huge mouth opened, engulfing almost half of her own young. Leaving the rest forever, she swam away through the pond water, surfacing in the shallow water near the arrowroot. She punctuated the silence with a loud croak of accomplishment.

Down from the dune sand, another baby snapping turtle made his way to the pond and home. Pausing not an instant at the water's edge, he flopped in, swimming forward. No bigger than a large coin, the young turtle swam

into the reeds to safety. There he stayed all day, eating nothing. Only yesterday he had been in the warmth of the sun-heated dune sand. Now he was in another darkness— the cold and wet of the pond, to which his cool blood adjusted without discomfort.

He did not want to move from his thicket of reeds, but he was prodded by want of food. Slowly he paddled through the surface water, coming to the eggs laid by the large female frog. He ate a number of them, slept, woke, and ate more. Some had already started incubating into tadpoles. These were meatier, less watery than the others. He found them delicious, and ate them zestfully. Rounding out his diet, he munched the edge of a lily pad.

His chewing was almost inaudible, so subtle was the sound of his gnawing. But the large cow frog heard it.

Moving swiftly through the pond with her long-legged kicks, she surfaced among the lily pads, only inches from him. The tiny turtle saw her head burst through and tried to dive downward, to escape, but it was too late. A large white mouth engulfed him, and once again he knew warmth and darkness. There was no pain, yet he struggled.

Inside her belly, the bullfrog's mate felt the feeble pecking of the tiny beak. Then he was still, as her digestive juices washed over him.

Twelve

Down in his hole under the toolshed, the pinto marmot was busily enlarging his burrow. The litter of five that his mate had delivered some months ago was making his quarters crowded. They were all more than half-grown, now that it was August. And seven marmots, all rapidly growing fur-thick for winter, made their main burrow less than adequate.

The male marmot, father of the brood of active whelps and head of his underground household, was in a nasty mood. August was warm—too warm to be digging in a fur coat. He halted his excavations, uttering a low whistle of fatigue. It was the same kind of whistle the man had made when he was digging the foundation for the toolshed.

He resumed his work. This time he found a vein where the earth was soft. His small paws worked like shovels. Suddenly he punched through a wall into a neighbor's dwelling. It was not yet evening, and the neighbor was very much at home. He repelled the marmot's intrusion with an orchestration of chattering, growls, scolding spits, hissing, scratches and bites. One bite in particular was made definite on the marmot's surprised nose as he poked it into his neighbor's den.

Indeed, the stoat was angry. Bad enough to have to have marmots next door, especially with five noisy brats. Now this. The stoat did not take kindly to an overt invasion of what he knew was his.

Modest though it is, a stoat's den is his castle. He had chosen the site (originally owned by a family of ground squirrels which he had driven away), replanned it, dug it, and furnished it. He would not abandon it because some clumsy woodchuck broke through a wall.

Although compared to the marmot an eight-inch stoat is tiny, he hopped to the point of entry, biting hard and screaming. The retreat of the big (and now quite sore) nose was prompt. The stoat snorted, repairing the gaping hole in his wall without further ado. It was doubtful that the marmot would stick *his* nose into stoat lodgings from now on.

Come evening, the stoat had put things right once again in his quarters beneath the tool shed. He would not move out of the area he had chosen. After all, he had been there first, and it was a good place to live. Very good, now that the boy in the house was trying to tame a young skunk. Every night he'd bring out bread and milk for it, which the skunk loved. So did the stoat, providing he could get to it ahead of his large black and white competitor. The stoat had a wiry weasel's tubular body (only an inch in diameter), and he was tough. But he was no match for a skunk. Few were. Except for the great horned owl, another character that the weasel meticulously avoided.

The stoat had another enemy close by. This one was larger than the skunk, and it was the boy's brown and white terrier.

Head first, with its ball-like muzzle, he peeked out of his burrow, then popped up. It was dark, but his long, furry, reddish-brown body glowed in the starlight. So did his creamy-yellow front, whenever he sat up (almost as a squirrel does) on his haunches to have a look around. His head was small, and his ears were placed flatly against it. The nose (his chief tool of detection) was constantly active, twitching with curiosity as it inhaled hunting information with every sniff. Under it, his mouth held a ring of thirty-four teeth that were highly respected by many in these parts. At least by the few who lived.

All clear. He ran in perfect register, hind feet stepping exactly into forefeet tracks. Bounding across the back lawn of the house, he looked like a rubbery garden hose making a series of S-like waves. His long, slender tail, half as long as his body, plumed behind him. On his short legs and tiny five-toed feet, he covered ground quickly and directly. Without fear he approached the back porch of the house. Ah, there it was! The little blue and white bowl of bread and milk. And there *he* was—the skunk for whom it had been set out.

The weasel hissed a warning, but it was ignored by the big, striped oaf. The skunk was a friendly fellow, and perhaps would have even shared his treat, but the stoat was not willing to risk it. He had been peppered once by a skunk several summers ago, and once was enough. He had made the mistake of thinking that a mild and pleasant nature means cowardice. How wrong he had been!

Weasels emit unpleasant odors, but they are fragrant compared to the powers of a skunk. Besides, this was not a young skunk, it was a mature male. And it was missing a toe or two on one of its hind feet.

With a snort, the stoat wisely decided that his thirst for milk sop did not warrant making himself a target for the skunk. Already the two sleepy, black eyes were fixed on him, even though the skunk calmly continued to lap up his snack. Among animals, as among men, awesome weaponry often preserves peace.

Leaving the back porch, the stoat scampered across the lawn, heading toward one of his favorite hunting haunts,

the tall timothy grass. But when he reached its outer edge, the brown and white terrier burst out of it, stepping on him. The male stoat was large, larger than the females in the area, but the terrier was the largest animal he had ever met.

The surprise of it all, coupled with the dog's weight on him, caused the stoat to do what weasel's seldom do—he panicked. Leaping into the open toolshed, he thrashed so hard that he knocked over some small flowerpots. He looked for a hole. There was none. The barking dog had chased him into the toolshed, adding to his confusion. Finding no downward route of escape, he turned. He was cornered, and so he faced the dog.

Curling his tiny lips, the stoat displayed two half-rings of sharp white teeth. Laying his tiny ears back flat against his head, he glowered upward from the toolshed floor at his noisy attacker. Cornered though he was, he could have darted to either side of the dog to freedom. But without hesitation, he hurled his small body at the soft fur of the terrier's throat.

Being stepped on earlier, the weasel had been surprised. Now it was the dog's turn. In the worst three seconds of his life, he was bitten over a dozen times. Rings of small teeth buzzed about his throat and mouth, tearing at the fleshy underlip. Opening his mouth in pain, he snapped again and again, trying to catch the stoat in his strong teeth where he could shake him, break his spine, and kill him. But the terrier's teeth only clicked together on emptiness. All of a sudden, the stoat was gone as fast as he had attacked. Out of the toolshed he went, diving into the night.

Five minutes later the stoat came across a young rabbit down in the meadow. It tried to escape, darting into a nearby hole. The weasel, being slightly smaller and sleeker, followed it underground with ease to the end of the burrow and killed it, sucking its blood to quench his thirst. Ripping it open, he fed first on the brain. Heart and liver followed, then the lungs. When he left the hole half an hour later little was left inside but fur, bones, and one foreleg.

Rabbits were plentiful in the meadow. On his way to the pond he killed another, leaving it entirely intact. He did not kill for fun. This was his role, as the official population controller of the area. It was an act executed swiftly and with the noble purpose of nature.

He scampered by the pond, running through the stand of maples. Climbing the rise, he stopped at the foot of the sweet gum tree. Of the many on the ground, he chose a golf-ball-size sweet gum ball, batting it alternately with his front paws. Lying on his back he juggled it, spun it, kicked it high in the air. And the moon could almost hear him laughing as he played.

Thirteen

All day long the sky had been gray.

The air was heavy with mist, and the wind blew in gusts for most of the afternoon. Toward evening it blew harder, so hard as to keep the bat from making her evening flight. She did not like the wind. It affected her hearing, her flying, and her hunting. So while the wind whined and groaned through the toolshed, she remained calmly on her favorite rafter, her wings drawn tightly about her, and her metabolism reduced to delay her hunger.

Her one offspring had long since left his mother and the toolshed. Now she was an old dowager and alone, but she did not care. She lived more quietly now, and hunted less. Little bothered her. Even when the wind pushed the bell in the toolshed cupola, she stayed unruffled throughout the long and rainy night.

Out in the meadow, a dead rabbit lay on its side. It had been killed by a weasel and left to feed the scavengers. But the scavengers had not come, except for a black ant or two. When the rain finally stopped, large paw prints were made near the remains of the dead cottontail. The prints were shaped much like a chicken drumstick—ball in front, elongating to a thin shank heel. It was an unusual print, unlike any other in the meadow or near the pond, because of its narrow length and wide toe span. In the mud, the toes spread to almost a webbing. In the snow of winter, the tracks of the great white snowshoe hare would be even wider.

He was not yet white. But as the weather cooled, as autumn came and went, he would whiten, as would the many others of his kind. Snowshoe hares are plentiful in winter, and as prey, they feed many a predator through the long night of cold and snow. They are rightly called "the bread of winter."

Rarely does a rabbit eat another rabbit. But the snowshoe hare is a scavenger, and this one was hungry. He did not like the rain and mist, but he was too hungry to remain in his shelter. His front incisor teeth tore into the belly meat of the dead cottontail. In his mouth the cold, partly rotten meat tasted good to him and gave him warmth.

Even before he heard the *hiss*, he was aware of her presence behind him. He turned to face her, wanting to fight, wanting to defend his right to the rabbit carrion. But a snowshoe hare, even a hungry one, is a poor match for a hungry opossum.

Her pointed snout curled back, showing sharp, pointed teeth. Her fur was gray-white—whiter at the roots, darkening at the tips. The opossum's ears were large for her face, almost bare of hair, like her long white tail. As she hissed at the hare to drive him away from the rabbit carrion, she dug her feet into the earth. She took a firm grip with the five digits on each of her feet. The large digit opposed the other four, and on it grew a nail instead of a claw.

This possum was hungry. She was very hungry, and ready to fight if need be. Shaped almost exactly like an enormous rat, she was two feet long, her tail adding another foot. Normally she weighed five pounds, but now she was pregnant, and thick with body fat.

She hissed again at him, showing her fangs, insistent that he surrender the remains of the dead rabbit to her. She was not in a mood to be patient about it.

This would be her second litter of the season. In late fall, there could be a third. Her constant state of expectation made her hunt often. To her, meat was meat, live or dead. She would not quibble about its freshness, any more than the big snowshoe she now faced.

Charging at him, she missed his throat, but her teeth buried in his shoulder. Twisting, he halfway threw her free, into a pose where he could club her with his great feet. Once! Twice! Both kicks were well aimed, the first crushing the soft tissues of her lip, the second pounding her flank and causing her breath to gush from her body. It was this second battering-ram kick that tore the slit entrance of her marsupial pouch. Again she hissed at him, and at her own pain.

But she was far from beaten. She leaped for a fresh hold on his head, and found it. Her teeth sank deep into his eye socket, forcing out his eyeball. This was her scoring shot at him, and he did not wait to see what else would come. One-eyed and bleeding, he released his hold on the carrion. In long bounding jumps, he fled. Blood was streaming from the place on the right side of his head that had once been an eye.

The possum was little better. Without being pregnant, it was bad enough to be kicked in the belly by a snowshoe hare; pregnant, it was double the pain. But at least another pain would soon be answered—her hunger. She had eaten little that evening.

She had awakened just at dusk. Being nocturnal, she did not leave her nest in the old, dead pine tree near the pond until it was completely dark. Briefly, she fed on the few remaining blackberries that she found, and a root or two. But the growing life in her belly demanded more.

It was raining, but somehow she dragged the dead cottontail down through the darkness to the pond. The dragging made a trail of crushed green blades in the wet meadow grass. Near the pond she stopped, breathing more heavily. Life kicked within her, but birth would have to

wait. Now she must eat. Her sharp teeth ripped into the ear of the rabbit, the ear by which she had dragged it. The meat pulp and cartilage were still moist inside. Bite after bite she wolfed the nourishment into her body. As she ate, she twisted her head sharply, trying to tear more meat from the carrion. Once her foot slipped on the mudbank, and it hit the edge of the water with a sharp slap. She ignored the sound, continuing to enjoy the dead meat. It was heard deep in the pond by the old snapping turtle, but he only widened his eyes briefly. It was nothing to interest him, since the slap wasn't followed by a helpless splashing. His senses weighed the sound, deciding it was an isolated noise and not a summons for him to kill and eat.

High in the oak tree, however, the great horned owl heard the slap made by the possum, and he was not in the least indifferent. He knew it came from the water's edge, and spreading his giant wings, he glided through the rain and mist down toward the pond, dropping over one hundred feet in only seconds.

By the time the possum had removed her foot from the pond and shaken it, before she had time to finish her rabbit (or even take one more bite), before she could make a retreat to her hollow pine tree and bear her litter of young possums, he came.

Massive talons opened, and closed on the gray-white fur of the possum's throat. The claws sank deep and would not release. Reacting that same instant, she pretended to die. Going limp, she pulled the owl backwards, down the wet bank and into the pond. The sky was his turf, but the pond was hers. As much as he hated the plaguing hunger in his gut, he hated the water more. It was a strange substance to him, not of his world. Water was not air and he could not cut through it with his strong wings, nor take it in his talons as he took life.

His beak opened in a screech as the weight of the possum in his claws pulled him deeper and deeper. Screaming, his head sank beneath the black surface. Like so many of his enemies, the great horned owl now knew panic. For the first time as a hunter, his talons relaxed. The grip on the opossum was released. All he wanted was air, not food. Beneath the dark water, he fought for surface. Once there, he fought as gallantly for shore. And more than his dignity was muddied as he slid and scrambled up the mud ooze to safety.

So the possum escaped her captor. It was most fortunate for her. Not often does a possum elude a great horned owl, especially a possum who is ponderously pregnant, and somewhat slowed from an earlier bout with a hard-kicking snowshoe hare. But she had survived, as possums have survived unchanged for a hundred million years. And so it was that in less than one hour, as she lay cold and wet and hurting in the pine tree, her labor began, and she gave birth.

The litter was large. Most of her litters were. This time she bore fifteen kits. As they popped from her like tiny links of sausages, she remained calm. One by one they left her birth canal, making their shaking, hungry way to the warm pouch on her belly. She did not assist them. Each kit fastened firmly on one of her twelve teats, to cling there for the first few weeks. The three that were the last to arrive found no teats unoccupied, and in less than a day, these three starved, and were eaten by the mother possum.

Two weeks later, she emerged from the hole in the dead pine tree. Clinging to her back were eleven young opossums. Number twelve rode in the rear, his long tail coiled tightly around his mother's. His eyes were open. By moonlight, he saw his first upside-down glimpse of the pond that would be his home.

Fourteen

Winter came, hardening the land.

Brown turned to white. And not just leaves to snow. The stoat was no longer brown—his fur was snow white, except for the tiny black tip of tail. The commoner became a lord; the stoat was now an ermine.

Evenings found him sliding down the white crust of the meadow hills, climbing up, and sliding again. It was more fun than juggling a sweet gum ball, more fun than killing a rabbit.

In the hole of the dead pine tree near the pond, the young possums were snug and warm, snarled together as they were. Outside, the wind was cold and fresh. Inside the dead pine, there was a strong smell of opossum. Close by, the pond was frozen, and covered by a light fall of new snow. Tracks marked the snow from one side of the pond to the other, most of them made by the boy and his dog.

There were other tracks. At first glance, they appeared to belong to a skunk, made by a pair of large, elongated hind feet and smaller, rounder front paws. But between the tracks was the lazy, S-like drag of a long, flat tail that was fringed with barby hair. It was not the tail of a skunk, nor his tracks, but the maker of those tracks possessed an odor that was almost skunklike.

A large vole had made the tracks. Like the opossums who lived nearby, he looked like a large rat. He was mature, and fourteen inches long, with a long flat black tail

that added another ten inches. He smelled musky, creating his own unique odor with a pair of tiny glands near his generative organs. These secreted a thick fluid that earned him his name—muskrat.

But as dismal as his smell was, his soft fur was handsome. Even wet, as he was now, poking his nose up through an air hole in the pond ice to breathe, his coat was a sturdy and shining armor. It was early winter, and he had not yet abandoned surface life altogether. It was a cold, clear winter night, and the muskrat blinked at the white moon that blued the snow.

Reaching his front paws up through the thin ice, the muskrat felt the rim of the air hole. The hole was larger than his usual breathing spots, because it was directly over a spring that fed the pond. Cautiously, he touched the snow with the hairless palms of his paws, his hind feet churning gently in the water. His hind feet were set at an angle to his leg, facing slightly outward to improve his swimming kick.

With a quick thrust of his body, he popped up through the hole onto the ice. He shook himself and sneezed, since there was water in his nose. In a quick trot, he crossed the pond to a stand of young sassafras trees. They were already winterbare, but as he nibbled one of the twigs, he could still taste a souvenir of aromatic sap that many such laurels have.

Holding the sassafras twig firmly by one end, he slid down a bank, crossed the pond and plunged into the water at the spring hole. Underwater, holding the twig in his strong teeth, the muskrat swam for sixty feet, to a dome-shaped lodge that stuck up over three feet from the surface. He and his mate had built the lodge in the fall. Each year there was a new one, as the rains and floods of spring usually washed the winter hut away. It was a simple mound of sticks, roots, mud, grass, and cattail stalks, with several doors, and a dry chamber in the center, just above the pond's surface. Several other mounds surrounded the main one, and served as shelters for food and feeding.

Inside the main chamber, he was greeted by the heavy smell of musk, and welcomed by his family—his mate, a new litter of three kits, and an earlier litter of four, now juveniles. The young ones greeted him with tiny, high-pitched peeps of recognition. Had he brought them the sweet stem of a water lily? Sassafras would do. With the exception of crayfish and freshwater mussels, the muskrats were content to be vegetarians and chewers of bark.

The younger litter still craved muskrat milk. They would not cultivate a liking for sassafras until the coming spring, when they would all be out of the lodge and living in the muddy bank, each entrance well hidden with a thatched door of ferns, grass, and leaves. But for now, it was winter, and under the ice of the pond, it would be a long, cold one. Perhaps even the air holes would close, iced in, and would require a fresh smashing each evening.

Several of the young muskrats rambled around their sire. One, a bit more zealous than his siblings, scored a deep bite on the mature muskrat's ear. This was not easy to do, since muskrat ears are tiny, and each pair is buried deep in the rich fur. The male opened his jaws, but did not bite back. He merely cuffed the small offender back into place. Rolling on his back, he let his offspring molest him, and each one joyfully rammed a blunt nose into his belly fur. At this he uttered not quite a giggle, but a happy, playful snort. He was mounded and mated for the winter and it was a good life, if often rough at times.

Winter was never an easy time, but it was a quiet one. Pleasures were more confined, and there was less swimming, less romping, and no sliding down the wet mudbank into the pond. Food was scarce, but if each muskrat slowed his system down enough, the food would last.

There were advantages to winter. Enemies, too, were confined—not restricted altogether, but reduced. The mink were not as fast in winter and neither were the martens. They weren't about to dive in the pond when it was December cold. Nor would the red fox. He came to the pond to drink at the airhole, but the wind blew into his fur, sending him back to the woods, and to the rock-pile hole where he had his bone-littered, feather-strewn den.

The great horned owl was high in his oak, and always hungry for a fat vole, from mouse to muskrat. But he hunted less in winter, ate less, heard less. Besides, flying fast through cold air watered his eyes.

Deep in the pond, another enemy slept. Come spring, the giant snapping turtle would be hungry again. A young muskrat would suit his taste. It was never wise for any muskrat to idle, kicking rings up on the surface of the pond, when from down in the depths he looked like a perfect bullseye to the giant snapper.

Winter did have its good side, even if the careful store of greens were gone by February, and the laurel bark was too tight to offer much nourishment.

The night lay ahead, so the male muskrat dived out of sight, into his living-room pool, down and out of his lodge, and across the pond. Once again he surfaced at the air hole made by the bubbling spring. He blew the water from his nose with a pronounced snort, and eyed the sky, listening intently for footfalls, his nose assuring him of safety.

Out of the air hole he shot, shaking water into the air about him. Following his earlier path, he ran toward the sassafras clump. Once there, he could not find a branch to please him. Several were too small, others were too old. First year growth was best—inside it was still green and ripe, and chewing it gave off a perfume that a bad-smelling fellow could savor. Perhaps if he tried another tree. This was his error.

An established food route from source to storage should not be changed. Before this his route had proved to be adequate; it was short, direct, discreet, and safe. The muskrat should have kept to it, trusted it, and remained faithful to it. A good path is a good friend.

But the muskrat wanted more. He jumped through the fresh, shoulder-deep snow. To his right was an area of packed snow where his travel would lighten. Reaching it, he pressed on toward another stand of sassafras. He did not bother to ask who had trampled the snow near the pond, or why. His only thought was of the new laurels ahead of him. It was then he heard the sound.

Clank!

At the same instant he felt a sharp pain cutting one of his rear legs just below the middle joint. It was a trap that the boy had set. The trap was laid open as a ring of toothed jaws, with a spot trigger in the center of the circle. The trigger was no larger than a silver dollar, and there was only one trap, but the muskrat had stepped on it, set it off, and now its jaws bit into his leg with pain enough to madden him. Using his sharp teeth he bit at the steel, which only hurt him more. His deft front paws, so artful at dabbing mud between the chinks of his winter lodge, tried to pry the jaws apart. But they were locked shut. Somewhere inside his leg, steel met steel; and the teeth were crushing his leg bone.

Again and again he bit at the trap, the rising pitch of pain spurring his madness. His mouth was bleeding, and the snow about him was spotting red. He tried another ruse. He would run from this spot, and drag the trap with him. But after two or three steps, the chain that held it to the base of a sassafras whipped taut, almost tearing foot from body. This time the pain was so intense he closed his eyes. In his rage, he had to bite something, sink his teeth into anything and gnaw his freedom.

Doubling his body into a ball, he bit into his own leg, higher up than where he was held by the trap. Again he knew the same pain that the trap had caused. As his teeth continued to gnaw his own flesh, he could no longer feel the trap jaws on his lower leg. But the new pain was worse. He was hitting nerves and tissues. Bite by bite, he ripped away his own leg flesh to expose the bone, but try as he could, his teeth could not snap it. His leg badly torn, he was losing blood faster now. The night seemed darker than it had been. The strength in his jaws seemed to weaken. He could not feel anything between them, anymore than he could feel any part of his foot and leg below the grip of the trap. He tried again to run, but the chain holding the trap to the tree would not break, and neither would his leg. Once more! And this time he was rewarded with the snap of bone. His leg was now fractured, but not cleanly broken. His teeth finished the break. Now he bled more; from his leg, and from the soft lips of his muzzle that were torn from a bone splinter.

Now he was free, yet he could not run. All he could do was crouch where he was in the bloody snow, his body trembling. Slowly his pain left him. Suddenly the hurt seemed to heal, until there was no pain. In his awareness there was no longer a trap with steel jaws holding bits of dark fur and the stump of a drained, whitening foot. There was no longer a torn leg. Neither was there a trip home. There were no kits, no mate to welcome him. No pond, no lodge, no moon.

Early the next morning, the boy and the dog were up before firstlight. Chasing each other they ran from the house across the lawn, past the toolshed, down the meadow to the pond. The boy was excited. This was his first trap. He was breathless to discover himself as a hunter. All the way to the pond, he and the dog unknowingly celebrated the running love of the chase, in all its glory.

The trap was closed. Its jaws had snapped shut, but it was empty except for the frozen remains of a foot and a few tufts of hair. The snow was trampled, and everywhere he looked the boy saw reddish-brown spots of dried blood. The terrier pup was busy, his perceptive nose telling him that there was more here than just a few toes. He worked his paws under some snow at the foot of a laurel, uncovering a small brown object and giving a yip of discovery.

Hurrying to see what the dog had found, the boy lifted the stiff, furry body up out of the blood-smeared snow, holding the muskrat in his arms. There was a slight tremble in his gut, as he knew the rapture and the regret of his first kill.

Fifteen

Winter softened into spring. The sun swelled big and strong, and the earth opened to be loved. April was aloof and running.

The terrier was a year older and no longer a pup. Barking less and smelling more, his soft brown eyes saw much that interested him, but little that alarmed him. No longer did he hunt by thrashing through the thickets of wild grape, but instead he measured each step with care. He had learned to hunt with little sound and little motion.

He made less racket, and with this quiet came a more mature bravery. He could wade into the pond and wait patiently for the riled-up black muck to settle before lapping the cool water, yet he respected true danger, such as the big snapping turtle, who would enjoy making a meal of his paw.

It was almost dawn, which made him stretch. He was anxious to be up and about, ready to start a new day. It was at this very moment that his ears snapped up and alert. Somewhere out on the meadow, a crow barked. It was not the crow's usual *caw caw caw*; this was different, a single stinging yap—a warning to all other animals that a predator was afoot or aloft. No matter which predator, from hawk to stoat, the crow felt it his duty to bark an alarm.

For a minute, all was still. The smaller creatures in the meadow froze at the cry of the crow. They read its meaning, as did the terrier. Those who could move quickly

dived into their burrows beneath the earth. Smaller ones scurried through their tunnels in the timothy. The only sound that the dog heard came from high in the willow tree, the chirp of an early rising whitecrown sparrow or skunkbird. He was the first to snap the spell of fear.

Across the back lawn and past the toolshed, the dog trotted down toward the meadow. If something big enough to alarm the old black crow was afoot, the dog wanted to learn more.

Lowering his nose to the ground, he smelled a bud of butterfly weed, starting to push its tiny stalk up through the sandy soil. Only minutes earlier, a small, gray meadowmouse had urinated on the butterfly bud, but the dog reacted without interest to the faint, acidy smell.

Scratching the dirt with his paw, the dog dislodged a

rock from its nest in the earth and discovered a sleeping salamander. Snout to tail, she was ten inches long, a very dark green with egg-yolk spots smaller than a dime. Her legs were delicate, showing that the salamander was a female.

She had wintered under the rock and was not yet awake. In the dark flesh of her rubbery side there was a deep depression, like a dent, where the stone's weight had pressed against her all winter. To the gentle nudge of his nose, she was cold and stiff to touch, even when he softly tapped her once with a careful paw. He let her sleep.

Moving through the dogbane, a tiny note or two of music made him stop. It seemed to come from the dunes near a juniper bush. The call was one very short blast and then a longer, climbing whistle, the call of the male bobwhite. The little quail was lonely and he wanted a mate. Chasing the whistle with his ear, the dog saw the bobwhite quail working on his nest deep in the timothy turned tawny by winter. The nest was complete, but the little quail was trying to make it even more soft and inviting. Hearing his note, a female would soon come to inspect it, and finding it to her liking (as well as its maker), she would stay.

The curious dog was about to move in when a stronger smell caught his attention—raccoon droppings. Late last night, he'd heard the snorting of two male coons, bluffing a fight over a female or over a territory—most probably the latter, since in the meadow, land was more prized than love. In a few weeks, softer sounds would be heard at the mouth of their den—the gentle purring made by the female coon to her kits.

The terrier had also heard the bark of a flying squirrel, on the way to his store of hickory nuts. Perhaps he might see her, as he had seen one last summer, carrying a fresh-picked bell of wild morning-glory to decorate her nest high up in the sweet gum tree. There she might be nursing up to eight young, lined up as tiny soldiers in two perfect rows to suck the eight teats that were buried in her belly fur.

The old black crow was right. A large hunter was indeed prowling in the meadow. Tiny pawprints had been made very recently in the soft earth, pawprints much smaller than the large ones of the mature terrier—the tracks of a red fox.

He walked with a slight stiffness in his left rear leg. Normally a fox walks as if he were two-legged, his hind feet stepping exactly into his front pawprints. This fox walked smartly on the right side, but the left side of his track was out of register, making the left print a hair larger than the right. The tracks in the mud were fresh. One print sank deep into the ground, and was now (as the terrier sniffed at it) slowly filling with water.

No longer could the lame old fox catch bobwhite quail or rabbits. Now he was a stalker of mating fieldmice, a digger of turtle eggs. But the wise black crow judged him to be a fox nonetheless, ten pounds of trouble and an enemy to warrant a warning caw.

The dog tracked the fox through the meadow to high ground. Here he spotted a modest pothole in the leaves, where the red fox had been so hungry he had unearthed a butternut. Bending close, the dog sniffed at some small leaflets that had begun to push up into the sunlight, tiny green hearts that would later flower out into purple violets.

Farther along, the tread of the crippled fox dived into a thicket of blackberry bushes. A sharp thorn still held a tuft of red fur, which whitened with every cool puff of morning wind. A strong gust suddenly tore it loose, and it wafted away.

Beyond the thicket, the fox tracks stopped at a crack between two rocks, where he had hoped a blacksnake might yet be asleep. As the dog tested the mossy crack cautiously, a damselfly darted out. Making a slight hum with her wings, she flew close. He raised his ears for an instant but did not bark; his nose was busy with red fox now, and a damselfly was dull by comparison.

Closer to the pond the earth was wetter, and the tracks of the fox sank deep into ground fresh with rain. Here and there, humps of meadow grass whiskered up from the mud, and in one of them had been a rabbit's nest. But now the doe was gone. She had borne her fawns here, yet only a few bones and some hair remained. Some bird tracks in the earth suggested that maybe the litter of young cottontails had been eaten by bluejays, or even by the black crow who had sounded the fox alarm. Smelling the nest, the dog felt no souvenir of warmth.

At water's edge, the still-wet shells of a pair of crayfish were lying on a flat rock. The fox had eaten, but a crayfish or two had been too modest a breakfast to heal the hurt in his belly. Possibly he had arrived too late for more than a bite of tender rabbit fawn, and as the old fox circled the pond he was still nearly empty. Walking probably hurt him—his footprints seemed to show a greater separation, indicating that he was now limping more. Yet he kept moving; the pain of hunger in his belly kept him going, and there would be no rest, no sleep, until somehow he made a kill. Despite the torture of each step, the hunter would still hunt. The fox was old or lame, possibly even both, but he was no quitter. He asked welfare of no one.

A few steps farther along, the dog could tell that the red fox had seen something. The tracks were slower, sinking deeper. He had stopped, waited, and then dashed headlong into a juniper bush. But there the dog found nothing, only a bent grouse feather lying nearby which told the story. The jaws of the fox had opened as he leaped, only to snap shut on nothing more than the tip of a wing feather. With a great drumming of wings, the partridge had roared away to safety, leaving behind only a broken feather, and a fox with an empty mouth, and an emptier belly. The crippled fox watched the grouse flap up and away, and all he could do was spit out a feather. His tracks went on.

As the dog stood in a clump of ferns, still laced with morning dew, he was bent on stalking the old fox. He had yet to catch one, or even run one down, and the idea of such pursuit pleased him.

It was then he heard it, the sound he heard each day— the whistle that meant more to him than any hunt or wild instinct. Bounding through the rain-soaked laurel bushes, water streaming from his flanks, he headed for the sound, running toward the whistle of his young master. As he ran he could see the boy. Ears back, he raced toward the small figure at the far end of the meadow that was waving to him under the yellow sky of morning.

His teeth chattered in the anticipation of their meeting. The day had come, and it felt good to have someone to love.

And he had the boy.

ROBERT NEWTON PECK comes from generations of Yankee dirt-farmers, which he calls "a dynasty of peasants." As a boy, he trapped, hunted and fished Vermont's Green Mountains and the Adirondacks. His *A Day No Pigs Would Die*, the story of a Vermont Shaker family, has recently been published by Knopf.

Robert Peck lives in Connecticut with his family.

BETTY FRASER was born in Boston and is a graduate of the Rhode Island School of Design. Now a resident of New York City, she is an enthusiastic plant raiser as well as an outstanding illustrator with many books to her credit.